THE ART OF 3-11s

AGE RANGE TOOLS FOR LEADING CHURCH-BASED GROUPS

Toolbag Contents

Index

3-11s. What a brilliant age group! They are eager to learn, absorb information like a sponge, ask endless questions, are enthusiastic about new experiences and have a great appetite for fun. Children in this age group are a challenge and often very hard work – sometimes our patience can be stretched to the limit!

Exhausting, yes, but well worth it! What an amazing opportunity to help children meet with God through the Bible and hear the Good News of Jesus in the process. Wow!

How the 'toolbag' works

The *Toolbag* series is designed to help you (and other leaders in your church) to explore an issue that is vital to your children's and youth ministry. In this 'toolbag', you will find practical help with running your group of under-11s and with being a confident leader.

You will have the opportunity to

 **see what the Bible says about leading, and explore the issue on your own or with other leaders**

 **pray about it**

 **get some off-the-peg, practical ideas**

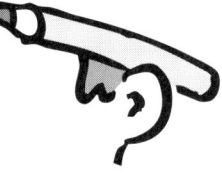 **make your own notes which will spur you into action**

 **hear real-life stories of churches that are working well with under-11s**

be reminded of what you have learnt in the Wow! boxes.

The right 'tools'

A toolbag has pockets which contain tools – that is obvious – but no toolbag does the work for you... at least we haven't found one yet that does! You will need to rummage through each 'pocket' to find exactly the right 'tool' for the job you have to do. So here are the 'tools' – the rest is up to you, to others in your church, and to God.

Need a hand?

If you are the only leader working with your group, you are still a team – with God. Try to set aside enough time, on a regular basis, to work through the 'toolbag'. Keep it somewhere visible with a Bible and pen, ready to dip into at any time.

If you do have other leaders in your team, make sure you meet regularly with them. You could use the material in one 'pocket' of this 'toolbag' as the first half of a meeting, with your normal planning and discussion handled much more quickly than usual in the second half.

Timescale

To guide you through the 'toolbag', some of the 'pockets' have a timescale attached to them. You need to delve into **Pockets 1, 2** and **3** before you start with your group, **Pocket 5** a few months after you begin and **Pocket 9** one year on. The other pockets in this 'toolbag' can be used as you need them.

The complete 'toolbag' will provide an invaluable training resource for your team, whether you are starting a brand-new group, inheriting an existing, well-established group, or simply feel in need of encouragement, inspiration and ideas. If you are already experienced as a leader, try using this 'toolbag' for your planning and training for a whole year, as a kind of refresher course.

Right now, build into your schedule time to sharpen up your leadership skills with *The ART of 3-11s,* at the appropriate times through the year. Perhaps mark in training sessions on your year planner, for yourself and your other leaders too, if you have them.

On the other hand, the suggested timescale might not fit with your situation. You may be told one week that you will be leading the group the next! In this case, simply use the Index on page 1 to pick out the 'tools' you need at any particular time.

Getting started

Make a date with yourself to dig into **Pocket 1** as soon as you can.

Alternatively, plan a time to get together with your other leaders. First, search through the 'pockets' yourself to select the 'tools' that will be most useful to you all.

We hope you will not only *survive* with your group, but thrive. God has plans for your leadership to be good news for you, your group, the church and, ultimately, the whole world. So go on, think big and enjoy it!

POCKET 1

PREPARING FOR THE TASK

If you have never been here before, welcome. If you have, welcome back. If you never went away, hello anyway! Perhaps you have picked up *The ART of 3-11s* saying, 'Well, I hope it tells me exactly what to do because I've never led a group before!' Or perhaps you are thinking, 'I wonder if this book will fit in with what I already know about children's work.' Whether or not you have been involved with children's groups before, you will find this 'toolbag' helpful.

Of course, there are many aspects of children's ministry which never change, but you may find some in this book which have not occurred to you before, or ideas which are new since you first started working with children. Perhaps working through this book will give you the opportunity to introduce new ideas and different ways of working with your particular age group.

WHERE ARE YOU GOING?

When you embark on a journey, it always helps if you know your destination, unless of course your name is Abram!

Below are some statements about the aims of church-based children's ministry. Whether your group is new or well established, it is always a good question to ask. With your leadership team, discuss each aim and tick those you agree with.

Then, individually, number them in order of priority, with '1' as the most important. Later, compare your answers and try to agree on a 'top three'.

Refer to Deuteronomy 6:6-7, 31:12 and Colossians 1:28-29 together, to see if there is any aim you should change, or move up or down your priority list. This will give you a basis for setting your own specific goals.

☐ To help children understand the Christian faith.

☐ To provide a Christian environment in which children can get together.

☐ To help children learn to pray.

☐ To help children understand the Bible.

☐ To help children become part of the church.

☐ To tell children Bible stories.

☐ To help children accept Jesus as their Saviour.

☐ To help children learn right from wrong.

☐ To help children worship.

☐ To play games and make things together.

☐ To give parents time and space to worship on their own.

☐ To help children develop as individuals.

☐ Because the church has always had a Sunday School.

☐ Because the children cannot understand, or be involved in, the church service.

☐ Other._____

_____

_____

How will you get there?

• Talk to your church leadership team and make sure they support what you propose to do.

• Put together a team of leaders. It is best to start by personally inviting people known or recommended to you and then, if necessary, appeal for volunteers.

• Consider the age range of the children who will come along – will you need to divide into small groups, or will you be able to cope with the age differences in one larger group?

• Discuss with parents matters such as programme content, the proposed venue and other outside activities which might clash. They are often the ones who pick up what the children really think!

• Do not be so busy preparing, that you neglect your own relationship with God – it is easily done!

YOU ARE UNIQUE

The unique combination of God-given gifts and abilities that you and your team members have is no coincidence and will help you achieve your aims. Some may not seem obvious at first, but could actually be very useful for children's ministry.

What can the team offer?

In the space below, identify the gifts, talents and skills which you can offer as a team.

Ask everyone to say what they really enjoy doing and what they think God may have enabled them to do or be. This needs to be handled sensitively.

Then **observe** each other and confirm these abilities, or suggest others. This process may take several weeks and you may want to review the situation together after seeing each other in action.

Now **pray** that all team members will recognize the spiritual gift or gifts they have – everyone has at least one (1 Peter 4:10).

Affirm each other sensitively as vital but different members of the body of Christ (1 Corinthians 12:27-31).

Mary – musician, encouragement, prayer.

Jo – teaching, writing of acetates, cooking.

_____
_____
_____
_____
_____
_____
_____
_____
_____
_____

As a guide, Romans 12:6-8, 1 Corinthians 12:8-10,28 and Ephesians 4:11 provide lists of spiritual gifts, but remember that the lists may not be exhaustive.

'It cannot be said often enough that what is needed is not primarily an expert... but above all a potent model for children of a Christian adult, with all the responsibility and opportunity that involves.'

(From *Children In The Way*, published by The National Society/Church House Publishing 1988)

Who is desirable?!

Of course, there is no such thing as an ideal children's leader. It is all about team work. We all have a lot to give. However, there are qualities which are desirable for all children's leaders. As a team, explore 1 Thessalonians 2:1-12 and 1 Timothy 4:9-16, then complete the list below.

Committed Christian.

Member of the local church.

Able to give time to meet with other leaders for planning and prayer.

Realizes the importance of building relationships with the children.

_____
_____
_____
_____
_____
_____
_____
_____
_____
_____
_____

WHAT ABOUT THE CHILDREN?

The Bible does not give us much specific advice about working with children, but it does show us what God thinks of them. In the Gospels we find several incidents of Jesus meeting children.

Children welcome!

Read through the following verses and imagine the scene taking place as though you are there. Look at what Jesus is doing and sense the reaction of the crowd around him. Imagine the reaction of the children as they come to Jesus and are valued by him. Be excited by the welcome that Jesus extends to the children and the high status he gives them in the kingdom of God.

'At that time the disciples came to Jesus and asked, "Who is the greatest in the kingdom of heaven?" He called a little child and had him stand among them. And he said: "I tell you the truth, unless you change and become like little children, you will never enter the kingdom of heaven. Therefore, whoever humbles himself like this child is the greatest in the kingdom of heaven. And whoever welcomes a little child like this in my name welcomes me."'

Matthew 18:1-5

A central place for children

'By drawing attention to children, speaking of them, healing them, commending them as examples and objects of care, Jesus handed to his followers a responsibility to give children a central place in their life together... A church which is faithful to its Lord will show its faithfulness in no clearer way than by its love for children, for whom he cared so deeply.'

(From *Children in the Early Church*, by W.A.Strange, used with kind permission of Paternoster Publishing.)

Get the church behind you

It is so important to have the support of the church for your work. To get you thinking about your church's attitude, look at the following statements and for each one mark a number on the scale according to whether you agree or disagree. Go on – enjoy a good generalization!

	Disagree			Agree	
Children are very welcome in our church	0	1	2	4	5
Children are considered important in our church	0	1	2	4	5
People in our church feel comfortable with children	0	1	2	4	5
Children in our church are happy to be there	0	1	2	4	5
People in our church understand how children develop in their thinking	0	1	2	4	5
People in our church understand how children's faith develops	0	1	2	4	5
People in our church would be willing to support children's work by praying	0	1	2	4	5
People in our church are keen to see children involved in corporate worship	0	1	2	4	5
Children are encouraged to join in other church activities as well as corporate worship	0	1	2	4	5

Shout about children

...in the most polite and sensitive way, of course! Obviously, if your *Get the church behind you* score was generally high, you have vital support from your church. If it was on the low side, you will need to educate your church members and help them to understand the importance of children's ministry.

Children's ministry needs prayer, encouragement and resources – it is part of the work of the whole church, a necessity not a bonus. It must be taken seriously. Children *must* be recognized as part of today's church.

So how can your church support your work? Firstly, make sure you have the full backing of your vicar or minister and that he or she shares your ideas about what should be happening. Secondly, keep other church members informed. Let them know how, when, where and especially *why* the children's work is organized, then let them know *who* it involves. Get people praying for the children and leaders by name.

Shout loudly! Talk to the church council, give a report in a Sunday morning service and have a feature in your church magazine or news sheet. Make sure the children are given a high profile. It may be tough going, but it will be worth it. Children are the responsibility of the whole church, and if everyone is involved in some way, everyone can share the reward of seeing God at work.

WOWc!

'What we invest in our own generation will die with us. What we invest in the new generation might still be there for our grandchildren.'

Penny Frank, Director of the Youth and Children Division of CPAS

In this 'pocket'...

you have considered

- your aims for doing children's work – keep thinking

- your gifts, talents and skills – keep praying and asking God to show you

- the characteristics of a good leader

- a little of what the Bible says about children

- some ways of giving the whole church the vision for children's ministry.

As soon as possible you need to talk to your other leaders about their gifts, and to your vicar, minister or children's work co-ordinator about your aims for children's ministry.

In the next 'pocket'...

you will think about

- child development

- the child's world

- handling the Bible with children.

If you have to wait a while before rummaging around in **Pocket 2**, don't worry, but do book in a session in which to do it.

If, as is more likely, you are so fired up already about your children's group that sleep can wait – **Pocket 2** is just waiting for you over on page 8!

POCKET 2

GETTING THERE

Hello again! Welcome to *Pocket 2*. This pocket will help you to make practical arrangements, to understand children better and to discover some really good ways of exploring the Bible with them.

NUTS AND BOLTS

First, here are some important things to sort out as soon as you can. If some are done already – great! Otherwise, tick each one as you do it or get it done.

☐ Talk through your aims with your vicar, minister or children's co-ordinator – just in case you didn't get round to it last month!

☐ Complete the gifts, talents and skills list for yourself and other group leaders (page 5).

☐ Inform all church members about the work you will soon be doing.

☐ Pray about the teaching session you will plan and the use of your gifts. Select teaching resources.

☐ If necessary, choose a name for your group and organise publicity.

☐ Find a suitable place for your group to meet.

☐ Discuss a budget for children's work with the church council.

☐ Talk with your team about any concerns, hopes or ideas for your group.

☐ Discuss your plans and swap ideas with the leaders of other age groups.

☐ Start inviting children to your group.

☐ Talk to parents about what will happen in your group – they will want to know.

☐ Beg, borrow or buy resources to use with your group, e.g. Bibles, crayons, paper, scissors, glue, stickers, pencils, percussion instruments, badges, overhead projector acetates and pens, a flipchart and paper, a cassette player, cassettes, and anything else you think will come in handy.

Remember – you cannot do all these jobs in one go and you do not have to do all of them yourself. Asking others to help – even those who are not part of your immediate leadership team – will give them the opportunity of being involved in the work.

WHERE ARE THE CHILDREN?

We shall never know exactly where children are in terms of their understanding of God and their relationship with him, but we *do* know that they will all be at different stages. This chart is based on observations by John Westerhoff and identifies four levels of faith development.

All different

We need to take into account the children's physical, social, moral and mental development. All of these will affect how we plan our sessions. What they can manage physically will influence our choice of craft activity; how they interact with peers will affect the games we play; and so on. But bear in mind that no two children are alike – because they develop at different rates, there may be huge differences in the ability and maturity of children of the same age.

FAITH DEVELOPMENT

Experienced faith During their early years, children's faith is associated with what or who is around them. Their experience of the trust, love and faith of others lays the foundations for their own faith.

Affiliative faith In childhood and early adolescence, children accept the beliefs of another person or group, either at home, school or church. They love to 'belong' and are carried along by others' enthusiasm. Experiences of awe, wonder and mystery are important to them.

Searching faith Often in later adolescence, religion of the head becomes as important as religion of the heart. Doubt and/or critical judgement come into play, as young people experiment with alternative understandings and ways. They need to be committed to persons and causes.

Owned faith People gain a personal faith that is expressed both in word and deed.

WHAT WHEN?

Look at the table below and the statements about the development of children. With your other leaders, decide which statements fit into each age group. Of course, some will go into more than one age group category. When you have done it, check your ideas against the information on page 10.

3-5 (pre-school)	5-7 (infant)	7-11 (junior)

Moral

1 wants to please
2 avoids blame and guilt
3 sees fairness as vital
4 has little sense of right or wrong
5 obeys rules to receive rewards

Mental

6 imitates others
7 asks questions to learn
8 adds, subtracts and reads
9 fantasy is less important
10 confuses the real and imaginary
11 learns best from physical activities
12 classifies, relates and orders
13 invents
14 recalls events

Social

15 self-centred
16 plays alongside rather than with others
17 enjoys being part of an organized group
18 eager to be accepted by children of the same age group
19 respects grown-ups

Physical

20 hand-eye co-ordination improves
21 runs, jumps and skips
22 has finer co-ordination – for example, can use scissors carefully
23 is restless when still
24 is conscious of appearance

Spiritual

25 experiences awe and wonder
26 imitates adult faith
27 asks 'why'
28 responds to the hero in a story
29 takes stories and symbols literally
30 may experience a vivid relationship with God

These categories are very general and there will be some overlap between the age ranges. However, they are a good, general guide to the development of children. Remember, though, that each child is individual and special. You are sure to know children who do not follow the pattern!

WHAT ARE THEY LIKE?

3-5

has little sense of right or wrong

obeys rules to receive rewards

imitates others

asks questions to learn

confuses the real and imaginary

learns best from physical activities

recalls events

responds to the hero in a story

self-centred

plays alongside rather than with others

respects grown-ups

invents

experiences awe and wonder

asks 'why'

takes stories and symbols literally

5-7

wants to please

avoids blame and guilt

obeys rules to receive rewards

asks questions to learn

adds, subtracts and reads

learns best from physical activities

classifies, relates and orders

recalls events

enjoys being part of an organized group

eager to be accepted by children of the same age group

experiences awe and wonder

respects grown-ups

hand-eye co-ordination improves

runs, jumps and skips

imitates adult faith

responds to the hero in a story

7-11

avoids blame and guilt

sees fairness as vital

adds, subtracts and reads

fantasy is less important

enjoys being part of an organized group

eager to be accepted by children of the same age group

has finer co-ordination

is restless when still

is conscious of appearance

imitates adult faith

may experience a vivid relationship with God

As you complete this activity, ask yourself the question: 'So how might these things affect the way I work with children?' For example, the fact that 3-7 year olds learn best from physical activities will mean that you plan practical sessions where they can use their bodies.

GETTING TO GRIPS WITH THE BIBLE

No matter what age group you are leading, you will want to explore the Bible with them. This is one of the most challenging and exciting things you will ever do as a leader. You will want children to get excited about the Bible and to start exploring it for themselves. This is an even greater challenge when you consider that your example of how to read the Bible may be the only one the children in your group will ever have as an example to follow.

The fullest possible picture

One of the hardest things to get right with the Bible is the meaning of a passage or story. Another is helping children see how it might apply to their lives. To begin to get to grips with these two skills, we shall look at the very well-known Parable of the Good Samaritan (Luke 10:25–37).

First we need to realize that the expert in the law, who approached Jesus, was a Jew (v25), and also that at the time Jesus told the story, Samaritans and Jews hated each other. Now read the story and let these two factors influence the way you respond to it. Imagine you are the expert in the law. How would you feel if a Samaritan cared for a fellow Jew? A Samaritan, the filthy swine – unbelievable!

'On one occasion an expert in the law stood up to test Jesus. "Teacher," he asked, "what must I do to inherit eternal life?"

"What is written in the Law?" he replied. "How do you read it?"

He answered: "'Love the Lord your God with all your heart and with all your soul and with all your strength and with all your mind'; and, 'Love your neighbour as yourself.'"

"You have answered correctly," Jesus replied. "Do this and you will live."

But he wanted to justify himself, so he asked Jesus, "And who is my neighbour?"

In reply Jesus said: "A man was going down from Jerusalem to Jericho, when he fell into the hands of robbers. They stripped him of his clothes, beat him and went away, leaving him half-dead. A priest happened to be going down the same road, and when he saw the man, he passed by on the other side. So too, a Levite, when he came to the place and saw him, passed by on the other side. But a Samaritan, as he travelled, came where the man was; and when he saw him, he took pity on him. He went to him and bandaged his wounds, pouring on oil and wine. Then he put the man on his own donkey, brought him to an inn and took care of him. The next day he took out two silver coins and gave them to the innkeeper. 'Look after him,' he said, 'and when I return, I will reimburse you for any extra expense you may have.'

"Which of these three do you think was a neighbour to the man who fell into the hands of robbers?"

The expert in the law replied, "The one who had mercy on him."

Jesus told him, "Go and do likewise."'

Luke 10:25–37

Leaders often teach children this story with the point that 'we should care for other people'. Jesus is actually saying much more than this. We should love *anyone* who is our neighbour, even if they are our enemies. When the expert in the law asks, 'And who is my neighbour?', he is thinking about the *minimum* he can do to be acceptable to God. Jesus' story shows him that living God's way is about doing the *maximum* – as much as we possibly can, to please him.

Exploring the Bible with children

With younger children, stories will help the Bible come to life, and there are plenty to choose from! However, although it is not so easy to explore, it would be a shame to ignore the rest of the Bible. The Psalms, the Prophets and the New Testament letters are all written in very different styles. So how can we be true to the Bible and really get to grips with what the verses are all about? One of the best ways is to ask the question 'What do these verses tell us about God and the way he wants us to live?'

Ideas for exploring non-story passages

Much of Paul's teaching is too difficult for young children to explore, but why not help them to **write** or **dictate a letter**, telling someone what they have learnt about Jesus? Then post the letters!

Play a game with the children which will help them understand more about the Bible verses. For example, running races will help the children understand the significance of Paul's words in Hebrews 12:1 about the Christian life being like a race.

Go for a walk to find a tree by a stream. This will help them understand Psalm 1.

Read a psalm together. Let the children close their eyes and listen to what the psalmist is saying about God. They could respond by drawing a picture, or writing their own psalm. Suitable psalms to use include 23,24,47,95,98 and 104.

Give older children who are familiar with the Bible, the following **symbols** to use: a lightbulb (for verses that shed light on something), a question mark (for things that need explanation) and an exclamation mark (for anything that they find amazing). Read the verses together and give the children a few minutes to note verses which fall into the above categories. Then discuss what they found.

The Adventure Begins

If you want a reservoir of innovative ideas for teaching the Bible in a way which really engages children and young teens, look no further than *The Adventure Begins* by Terry Clutterham (published by CPAS and Scripture Union, 1996). It is full of creative ideas and practical suggestions for different ways of exploring the Bible with children.

What about children who find reading difficult?

The Bible can be a daunting book for anyone, but especially for children who struggle with reading. They may not yet have learnt to read, or may have a specific problem, or may simply find reading a bore. Watch out for children who have difficulties.

Read *to* them if necessary, rather than expecting them to cope with reading the text for themselves – after all, the page layout is very different to an ordinary book. Keep any printed text they *do* need to read as short as possible and allocate an adult to help them follow the words as they are being read.

Be imaginative in the way you present the Bible. Use videos or re-tell the story in your own words. Pictures and symbols can help children focus on the meaning of verses. Read a story with pauses, letting the children supply the missing words. Involve them physically and get them to participate with actions, expressions and cheering, if appropriate. Songs, raps and rhymes can help children understand a story. Drama, mime, puppets or a photo story will really bring the Bible to life. Quizzes can reinforce the message.

Be as creative as possible and it will help everyone to appreciate and learn from God's word, whether or not they can read it for themselves.

Be a culture vulture

Everything we do with children is affected by the world in which they live. Children will measure the activities we organize for them against their cultural experiences in other areas of life. So if you understand something of the world in which the children live, it will help you to plan and prepare at the right level. Use the chart below to check what you know about current trends.

Are you in touch?

Circle the number to show how many you can name in each category. Think particularly of the age-group you are working with.

Toys with which children currently play

0 1 2 4 5 more than 5

Current children's TV shows

0 1 2 4 5 more than 5

Bands to which children currently listen

0 1 2 4 5 more than 5

Books or magazines that children currently read

0 1 2 4 5 more than 5

If you answered '1' or more to any of the above, write here what they are called – just to prove that you're not kidding yourself!

Toys_____

_____

_____

TV shows_____

_____

_____

Bands_____

_____

_____

Books or magazines_____

_____

_____

If you came up with some names, well done! If not, try to find out how children are filling their time. If you have children of your own, nephews, nieces or godchildren, talk with them about what they like and why they like it. Ask children in your church what they watch on television, or play with at home.

However, not all children will be interested in current trends to the same extent. Many will not be able to keep up with popular trends or latest fashions, perhaps because of financial restrictions at home, so it is important to find out what each individual child is interested in, and not to make assumptions.

All we need

Food in our bellies
Hats on our heads
Water to quench us
Sheets on our beds.

Teachers to teach us
Shoes on our feet
Trousers and t-shirts
Shelter and heat.

Someone to love us
Someone to love
Hope for the future
Light from above.

(From *The Day I Fell Down the Toilet* by Steve Turner, published by Lion Publishing plc, 1996.)

POCKET 3

ON WITH THE JOB!

It can be very daunting to think about putting together teaching sessions to help children learn more about God. Essentially, the purpose of children's work is not to fill their heads with facts – although everyone will gain knowledge as you learn together – but to help them know and serve God.

BECOMING PERFECT

Colossians 1:28 keeps us focused on the aim of our teaching and learning:

> 'We proclaim him [Christ], admonishing and teaching everyone with all wisdom, so that we may present everyone perfect in Christ.'
>
> Colossians 1:28

God wants the children *and* adults *(everyone)* in our group to be mature and to grow into perfection in Christ. Our group needs to be a place where this can happen. Gulp!

Life-related learning

What we share with children must relate to their lives and connect with something familiar to them. For example, our teaching about prayer should relate to children's chief concerns and help them to develop their relationship with God. Our teaching and learning will make the greatest impact if they can see how it might apply to their lives at home, at school, with their friends and in church.

All-engaging learning

Secondly, we need to make sure that, in our teaching sessions, children are

- enjoying being part of the group
- interested in what they are doing
- challenged by what they learn
- encouraged to keep following Jesus.

Decide which teaching materials to use or, perhaps, whether to use any at all. There are many resources available which give you a programme to follow with activities, take-home sheets, ideas for games and photocopiable material to use in group sessions. Your local Christian bookshop should have a range of suitable materials. Good resources to investigate include those produced by CPAS, Scripture Union and The Bible Reading Fellowship (see *More Tools* on page 48).

Several factors may influence your choice: the age group for which you are responsible, the amount of preparation necessary for each teaching session and, of course, the type of activities included.

BUZZ ABOUT STYLE

With your other leaders, spend time talking about how you would like the group to operate. For example, will your group have a relaxed feel about it or be very structured? Will you want to keep the format similar from one week to the next or change things around each time? Try to answer these questions from the children's point of view as well as from your own. For example, if you were a child, what would you like to see happening as you enter the room ready for your teaching session? What would you enjoy doing with other children?

Decide on a teaching style with which *you* feel comfortable, but also consider the children, and balance their needs against yours.

EVALUATING DIFFERENT METHODS

Think how successful these teaching methods might be with your group.

	Input	Example activity	Outcome
Method A			
Method B			
Method C			
Method D			

Method A

The leader talks about a subject.

Listening.

The children remember and understand with varying levels of success.

Method B

The leader talks to the group about a particular subject, such as following Jesus.

The children play a game for which they are blindfolded and have to follow a partner.

The children learn from comparison between following their partner in the game and following Jesus.

Method C

Brief input beforehand, such as a discussion about prayer and what the Bible says about it.

Writing prayers and/or praying together about issues suggested by the children themselves.

The children learn from doing the activities and making them part of their life.

Method D

Short introduction to a subject, for example by asking the question 'How can we follow Jesus?' and listening to children's ideas.

Lots of related activities, such as playing a game, listening to a Bible story, doing drama or drawing a picture.

The children are helped to recognize what they have learnt from doing the activities.

Methods B, C and D are the most commonly used in children's groups; Method A is really the way a sermon works – not ideal for children!

Planning a learning session

Imagine you are planning a 45-minute session for a group of 5-7 year olds about Jesus calming the storm (Mark 4:35-41). You need to keep the children active and not let anything last too long, or they will get bored. So you could use a game, a song, some drama, a story, a craft activity, some prayers and a news feature. There is a possible outline over on page 16.

1 (5 minutes) As the children arrive, give them a simple jigsaw of a boat to piece together.

2 (3 minutes) Discuss what was on the jigsaws. Who has been in a boat? When? Where? What was it like?

3 (6 minutes) Play 'Working on the Ship'. Talk about jobs to do on board a ship, such as cleaning the decks and putting up the sails. The children start miming different jobs. When you shout 'The Captain's coming!', they must stand to attention, completely still. Anyone the Captain sees moving becomes a Captain with you, so no one is 'out'. The last sailor to be caught moving is the winner.

4 (6 minutes) Tell the story of Jesus calming the storm. Ask the children to provide the sound effects of the wind and waves, getting quieter as the storm dies down. Perhaps read the story twice, making the first time through a practice.

5 (2 minutes) Discuss how the disciples in the boat might have felt.

6 (4 minutes) Now tell the story in a way that helps the children to be 'in' the story themselves – 'You are sitting in the boat when you hear the wind blowing. You look up at the sails and see that they are beginning to flap violently. You all jump up and try to get the sails down. You pull very hard...'

7 (4 minutes) Ask what it felt like to be in the boat. What was it like when Jesus stopped the storm? Talk about Jesus being powerful because he is God. What difference does it make to us that he is so powerful?

8 (8 minutes) Make a business-type card or bookmark for each child to complete. On one side it says, 'When I am frightened of... I can ask Jesus to help me'; on the reverse, 'Who is this man? Even the wind and the waves obey him' (Mark 4:41), for the children to learn as a memory verse.

9 (3 minutes) Sing a song about having Jesus to help us, such as *With Jesus in the boat we can smile at the storm.*

10 (3 minutes) Pray about times when we feel frightened.

This session involves a lot of activity, none of which lasts long. Ten separate activities in one session may be too many, but it is better to plan too much than not enough – you can always save something for another time. All the suggestions above could be done in one large group with the children all together if necessary, but if possible, split them into smaller groups with an adult leader per group.

It could be part of a series called 'Who is Jesus?', and you could adapt it in the following ways for use with older or younger children:

• Have easier or more difficult jigsaws to put together.

• If the session feels too long for younger children, omit the sound-effect version of the story.

• When you talk about the Bible verses, ask older children what it tells us about Jesus. Can they think of words to describe him?

• Instead of the business card or bookmark, younger children can draw and colour a worried face on a paper plate to show how they feel when they are frightened. On the other side they could draw a different expression to show how they will feel when Jesus helps them.

Structuring a session

Bear in mind the outline for Jesus calming the storm, as we examine the structure of a session. Here is an example of a structure that works, but there are others, so be open to suggestions!

1 Activity for the children to do as they come into the room, such as a puzzle or wordsearch.

2 Activity which fits the theme of the session, such as a trust game in which the children lead a blindfolded partner around the room and talk about how it felt afterwards.

3 Discussion about the day's session, using questions such as 'What things make us afraid?' and 'What is it like to go somewhere new?', and leading into...

4 Bible story, such as the Israelites crossing the Red Sea (Exodus 14).

5 Activity, such as drawing a cartoon strip that shows the Israelites crossing the sea.

6 Thinking about the story – 'Why were the Israelites afraid?', 'How did knowing that God was with them help the people?', 'Would *you* have trusted God, if you had been there?'

7 Application of the Bible verses to the children's lives. Encourage them to think how what they have learnt can make a difference to the way they live (for instance, 'God keeps his promises and leads his people; he will do this for us too; what do *we* need God's help with just now?'). Do not be afraid to share your own needs with the children and tell them how God helps *you* through his word.

8 Response to God, for example by singing about trusting him, by praying for each other or by having a time of quiet in which to ask God to help us trust him more.

Brighten up your sessions

Consider some of the following ideas for developing your programme:

• a theme such as 'prayer', 'Jesus' life' or 'God's world';

• craft activities such as making cards to give to new church members or creating a nativity scene to place in church;

• fun, 'getting to know you' activities such as walking to the park, making cakes or doing a sponsored event to raise money for a Christian relief agency;

• an invitation session such as a Bring-a-Parent morning;

• input from outside visitors such as a member of a missionary organization or a church member;

• a simple aerobics or keep-fit session for times when the children need to let off steam!

'I like it when we do cooking in Sunday School... I like playing with the plasticine...'

Darren and Michelle, aged 7

'...it's a fun way to learn about God. It's cool.'

Kirsty and Lucy, aged 8

We are not teachers and the children are not pupils – we are *all* learning more about God – together!

Plan sessions with a different feel. Children do enjoy variety, although they also like the security of a routine, so keep some of the same activities each week. Take a few risks and try new ideas, you can always drop them if they flop! Work hard at building relationships with your group. The better you know your children, the more enjoyable and fruitful your time together will be.

Plan, prepare and pray

Here are some suggestions for planning teaching sessions effectively:

• Meet the other leaders of the group to plan, prepare and pray. This will stop you putting it off!

• Get a routine going from the beginning so that meeting together as soon after the last teaching session as possible, becomes a fixed part of your week. That way you can de-brief before you plan.

• If you cannot meet straight after your last session, try to get together several days before your next one. Planning the night before can result in hastily-put-together sessions and tired leaders!

This kind of timing will also give you the opportunity to think things through and make changes before it is too late.

POCKET
4

GOOD, SAFE PRACTICE

The safety of the children in our care must be a top priority for us. This means taking into account the requirements of *The Children Act*, the aim of which is to help keep both children and adults safe as they work together. This is not an 'optional extra' in children's ministry which can be ignored or left until a later date – it is a matter of extreme urgency which needs to be handled sensitively and responsibly *now*.

As we think about the children in our care and how we can protect them from harm, use the words of this well-known hymn as a prayer on behalf of the children.

Christ be with me, Christ within me,

Christ behind me, Christ before me,

Christ beside me, Christ to win me,

Christ to comfort and restore me.

Christ beneath me, Christ above me,

Christ in quiet, Christ in danger,

Christ in hearts of all that love me,

Christ in mouth of friend and stranger.

(From *St Patrick's Breastplate*, translated by C.F. Alexander.)

THE CHILDREN ACT 1989

The Children Act 1989 is the most far-reaching reform of child care law this century. It contains implications for all those working with children under eight years old, both in the public sector and in voluntary capacities. The guidelines are designed to support good, safe practice and to encourage the best possible work with children. Following these guidelines will ensure safety for children and will protect leaders in their work as volunteers.

In July 1995, the House of Bishops issued a policy statement on child abuse and listed its recommendation for safe practice in children's and youth work. It follows the Home Office Code of Practice *Safe from Harm* which focuses on the work of voluntary organizations. The House of Bishops recommends that every church council buy a copy of this document and follow its thirteen guidelines. Most diocesan offices have also prepared their own guidelines on this issue (contact yours for further information).

Whilst *The Children Act* only legislates for work with those aged under eight, we firmly believe that all work with children and young people should be of the highest possible standard. So please see the following recommendations as ways of attaining this high standard for children of all ages. Failure to take the necessary steps could open church councils to a claim of negligence if a child or young person comes to harm at the hand of anyone working with under-18s.

Personal declaration form

The House of Bishops' *Policy on Child Abuse* requires that all those working with children and young people should sign a personal declaration form. There is a copy of this form on page 20. Please copy and use it. Always ask new leaders for a reference. Use the following notes to guide you through this sensitive process:

1 When using such a form with other leaders, emphasize that it is a positive action for good practice and should in no way be considered as an implication of slur or suspicion. Link the use of the form with other issues of good practice. It is as fundamental as having a clean and safe physical environment for children.

2 The nature of the form is obviously sensitive and should therefore be handled with care. Never hand it out without explanation. It may well arouse different emotions both in leaders and also in other church members.

3 Ask for it to be completed and returned promptly. If possible, work through the form *with* potential leaders or explain its use to a leadership team as a whole.

4 Ensure that confidentiality is maintained. In accordance with the *Data Protection Act*, do not give any information to third parties.

5 If any answer is 'Yes', allow the individual to explain this disclosure personally or by letter. If you are in any doubt regarding the individual's suitability for leadership, consult your Bishop's Representative on Child Protection. All dioceses should now have someone appointed to this position.

6 As well as the declaration form, it is recommended that new leaders offer one name as a referee for

them. Questions that could be asked include:

• In what capacity have you known the applicant and for how long?

• How willing and able is he/she to work with others?

• How suitable would you consider him/her for work in the... age range?

• (Mention the points listed below as guidelines for selecting leaders.) Are there any of these areas which may cause you concern about the applicant?

7 Following *The Children Act*, it is recommended that employers involved in children's work should take certain factors into consideration when appointing leaders. Similarly, churches should consider the same points. They are not compulsory, but are a useful guide for good practice.

◗ Some previous experience of children's and youth work is desirable, although not compulsory. If applicants have no experience or training, a willingness to undertake some sort of skills development is desirable.

◗ Leaders should be able to provide 'warm and consistent care' and be willing to 'respect the background and culture of the children and young people in their care'.

◗ Leaders should be committed to treating all children and young people as individuals, with equal concern.

◗ Leaders should have reasonable physical health, mental stability, integrity and flexibility.

CONFIDENTIAL DECLARATION FOR CHILDREN'S LEADERS

Confidential

This form is to help you, the children's work organizers, and the parents of the children attending our activities to have every confidence in the care we shall provide. It is in no way a comment or judgement on your qualities, but will be completed by all leaders. If you have any questions about it, please direct them to

_____ (name of supervisor)

_____

Guidelines from the Home Office following _The Children Act 1989_ advise all voluntary organizations, including churches, to take steps to ensure the safety of children in their care. We would like to take notice of this advice for our young people's groups too. In accordance with the House of Bishops' _Policy on Child Abuse_, you are therefore requested to make the following declaration:

Have you ever been convicted of a criminal offence (including any 'spent convictions' under the _Rehabilitation of Offenders Act 1974_) or been cautioned by the police or bound over to keep the peace? (1)

☐ Yes

☐ No

If 'Yes', please state the nature and date(s) of the offence(s), continuing on a separate sheet of paper if necessary.

Have you ever been held liable by a court for a civil wrong or had an order made against you by a matrimonial or family court?

☐ Yes

☐ No

If 'Yes', please give details, continuing on a separate piece of paper if necessary.

Has your conduct ever caused or been likely to cause harm to a child or put a child at risk, or, to your knowledge, has it ever been alleged that your conduct has resulted in any of these things? (2)

☐ Yes

☐ No

If 'Yes', please give full details, including the date(s) and nature of the conduct, and whether you were dismissed, disciplined, moved to other work or resigned from any paid or voluntary work as a result. Please continue on a separate sheet of paper if necessary.

Signed _____

Date _____

Notes

(1) Because of the nature of the work for which you are applying, this post is exempt from the provision of Section 4(ii) of the _Rehabilitation of Offenders Act 1974_, by virtue of the _Rehabilitation of Offenders Act 1974 (Exemptions) Order 1975_. You are therefore not entitled to withhold information about convictions which for other purposes are 'spent' under the provisions of the Act and, in the event of appointment, any failure to disclose such convictions could result in the withdrawal of approval to work with children or young people in the church.

(2) a: A child for this purpose means anyone under the age of eighteen.

b: 'Harm' includes ill-treatment of any kind (including sexual abuse) or impairment of physical or mental health or development.

c: This question relates to any conduct, whether as a paid employee, a voluntary worker, or otherwise.

Further essential safety guidelines

Leader to child ratios

The Children Act recommends the following ratios of leaders to children according to their age:

For 0 to 2 years: 1 leader to every 3 children (1:3)

For 2 to 3 years: 1 leader to every 4 children (1:4)

For 3 to 8 years: 1 leader to every 8 children (1:8)

For over-8s: 1 leader for the first 8 children (1:8), followed by 1:12.

Leaders and groups

In addition to the ratios above, please ensure that there is always more than one leader for a group of any size. If possible, have at least one male leader and one female if the group is mixed.

Leaders alone with children

Leaders should minimize the amount of time they spend alone with a child. If it is vital to be isolated with an individual, ensure that another leader is informed of where you will be and why. If possible remain in the view of another leader. Try never to be behind a closed door.

Registration of premises

If you run an activity for more than two hours in any one day or you run a holiday club for six days or more in a year, you must register your premises with your local Social Services. They simply keep a list of where and when activities run. There is usually a small fee for registration. The law presumes that registration will be granted unless there are good reasons why it should not be. You will find the telephone number of your social services in the phone book.

For most children's groups which run for less than two hours (for instance, during a Sunday service), the following requirements are not compulsory but they are a good guide to follow.

Space

Make sure you have enough space for the number of children in your group. You need 2.3 square metres per child of *unencumbered* space, that is, with no stacks of chairs or other furniture in it.

Toilets

The ideal is one toilet and one hand basin for every ten children. Try to avoid the use of roller towels.

Play area

Outdoor play space is recommended when an activity runs for more than four hours. A quiet play area is also valuable.

Warmth and cleanliness

Group areas should be warm, adequately lit and ventilated. Maintain high standards of cleanliness.

Food preparation

If you are preparing food on site, the area will have to be checked by the Environmental Health Office. If children bring sandwiches, ideally they should be refrigerated. Drinks must be available at all times.

Special needs

Be able and willing to accommodate children with special needs. Be aware of access to your building and toilet facilities.

Health and safety

Always have access to a phone on the premises. (This could be a mobile phone.)

Adults must be aware of safety and fire procedures. A fire drill should be carried out regularly. Fire extinguishers should be available and regularly checked.

Children with infectious illnesses must not attend.

Smoking should not be permitted near the areas in which children will operate.

Children should submit a health form before an activity, with brief details of any allergies or medical conditions such as asthma or diabetes. Take health forms when going off-site.

Accidents should be recorded, with a note of any action taken and signed by the leader involved. A first-aid kit should always be available and its location well known. No medication should be administered without written parental consent. One leader should ideally be a first aider.

Administration

Keep an up-to-date register and record of children, their parents (and contact phone numbers), attendance and other specific information such as whether they have asthma, epilepsy, diabetes or allergies. A register must be kept and be easily accessible in an emergency. The sample record card on page 35 will give you a shape with which to work.

Insurance

All groups need public liability insurance against a court awarding compensation for damage and also against someone suing a leader personally, rather than the church. Make sure your church's policy covers all your activities both on and off site. Check it with your church leader, administrator or treasurer.

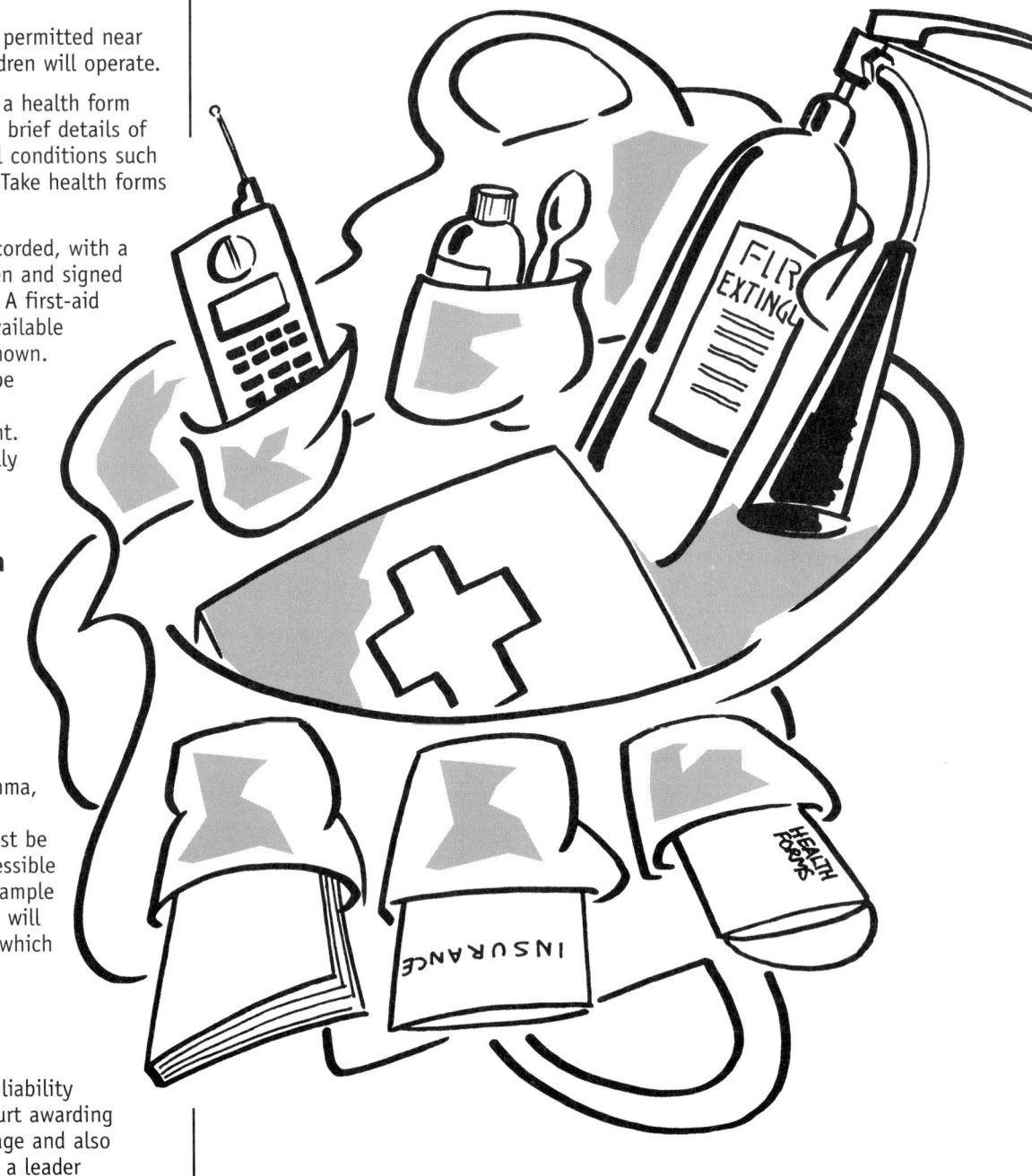

POCKET 5

SHARPENING UP

Are you beginning to feel that the hard work of planning and praying is bearing fruit? Or do you feel overwhelmed? If you do, it is quite normal, and most people do at some point. After all, we are engaged in a spiritual battle, and we will face opposition in different ways, just when we do not need it!

What should she do first?

'Why on earth had she said "Yes"? Wasn't a new job, new home and new church enough, without landing herself back into children's work? Mary had been determined to give herself some space, but the appeal in the notice sheet for a new leader was so desperate and the idea of the group being closed, unbearable.

Now she just didn't know what to do first; mark the pile of school project files, make new curtains, prepare for the group or maybe... emigrate!'

If things are not going entirely smoothly in your group, do not panic! Problems occur in every church, no matter how experienced the leaders are. There is nothing wrong with admitting that things are not perfect. Difficulties may occur because of a number of factors such as group size, age differences, family background or very lively children – they are common problems, so do not worry!

Remember that large numbers of children are not necessarily an indication of success – your work may be just as effective with a small number of children who come to your group week after week. Jesus concentrated on a group of just twelve friends, even though he also had a larger group of followers.

Some problems will disappear once your group is established; others will take a while to work through. You cannot do everything at once. Talk to your other leaders about the difficulties so that you do not feel you are facing them alone. Pray together about them, and be specific. It will help!

Brainstorm ideas for ways of dealing with the problems and your church leader for advice too.

Stay determined!

Determination to keep going is one of the most vital attributes of a children's leader!

'Not that I have already obtained all this, or have already been made perfect, but I press on to take hold of that for which Christ Jesus took hold of me. Brothers, I do not consider myself yet to have taken hold of it. But one thing I do: Forgetting what is behind and straining towards what is ahead, I press on towards the goal to win the prize for which God has called me heavenwards in Christ Jesus.'

Philippians 3:12-14

STAY IN TOUCH

At this stage, you may find it more difficult to step back from the week-by-week planning and running of the group, to see where you have come from and where you are going. Difficulties can begin to arise when we fail to do this regularly. In this 'pocket' we shall try to make sure this happens by 'staying in touch' with the children in our group, with their families, with the rest of the church, with our other leaders and with ourselves.

IN TOUCH WITH THE CHILDREN

In the early stages of your group, one of the most important things to do is build good relationships with the children.

The story so far

Take a few moments to think about what has happened during the first three months of leading your group. Circle a number between 1 and 5 against each statement. '1' means 'I strongly disagree' and '5' means 'I strongly agree'.

I know the children well

0 1 2 4 5

We celebrate their birthdays

0 1 2 4 5

The children are keen to learn

0 1 2 4 5

I can tell that the children are learning a lot about God

0 1 2 4 5

I am learning a lot about God from them

0 1 2 4 5

I feel comfortable with leading the group

0 1 2 4 5

The children feel comfortable to talk about themselves

0 1 2 4 5

The children enjoy coming to the group

0 1 2 4 5

I can see signs of growth in them

0 1 2 4 5

Sometimes I am able to tell the children about what God is doing in my own life

0 1 2 4 5

The teaching resources seem to suit them well

0 1 2 4 5

Discipline is not a problem

0 1 2 4 5

I have begun to get to know the children's families

0 1 2 4 5

Building relationships

Think of one child in your group and write down as much as you can about him or her. Include details of what they look like, reaction to different situations, sense of humour, likes, dislikes, and hobbies.

Perhaps you will realize there is a gap in your relationship with this child. Here are some suggestions for getting to know the children in your group better:

• **Listen** carefully to all they tell you about their home, school, friends and pastimes. Try to refer to the details in these comments some time during the following session.

• **Plan** sessions which include time to get to know them, for example, making cakes or playing games.

• **Answer** the children's questions honestly.

• **Be interested** in what the children find fascinating.

• **Make time** for one-to-one conversations with the children.

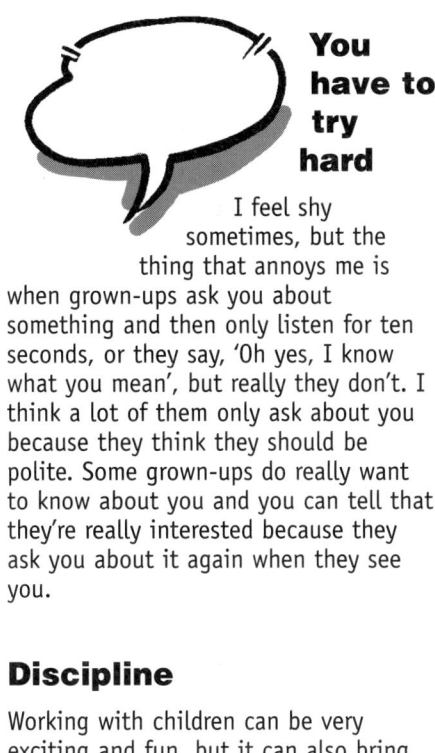

You have to try hard

I feel shy sometimes, but the thing that annoys me is when grown-ups ask you about something and then only listen for ten seconds, or they say, 'Oh yes, I know what you mean', but really they don't. I think a lot of them only ask about you because they think they should be polite. Some grown-ups do really want to know about you and you can tell that they're really interested because they ask you about it again when they see you.

Discipline

Working with children can be very exciting and fun, but it can also bring problems. Sometimes we shall struggle to get them to do what we want them to do, or to behave as we feel they should.

Do this activity with your other leaders so that you can support each other and offer alternative ways of dealing with tricky situations.

What do you do when a child...

☐ will not stop shouting?

_____

_____

☐ will not sit down and listen to what you are saying?

_____

_____

☐ will not join in with an activity?

_____

_____

☐ will not leave you alone (for instance, will not let go of your hand)?

_____

_____

☐ breaks or 'steals' things that other children are trying to use?

_____

_____

☐ deliberately hurts another child?

_____

_____

☐ looks around the room at something else while you are telling a story?

_____

_____

It is often hard to know the best thing to do in a particular tricky situation – we sometimes find out only by trying it! However, here are some tried-and-tested strategies:

• Try to have a good leader/child ratio. Consider allocating a leader to a difficult child as a 'minder' if necessary. It can end up being a bonus, as that leader will often build up a rapport with the child.

• Think about the routines involved in your group. How do the children come into the room? Is there something for them to do or anywhere for them to sit while everybody arrives? Is the atmosphere calm and welcoming? Lively background music can actually wind children up unhelpfully, making control and the focus of their attention hard to gain.

• If you split the children into smaller groups, think about what will happen if some finish earlier than others.

• Make sure the children are well occupied. Have a few activities 'up your sleeve' for emergencies.

• Think about your own example. If _you_ shout, why shouldn't the children?

• If a child shouts, try to keep your voice low as you respond.

• Avoid confrontation. Deal with specific incidents away from the rest of the children, but in full view of other leaders.

• If you feel you can ignore a particular incident, do.

• Removing children temporarily from a situation in which they are misbehaving may calm them down and help to defuse the situation.

Glimpses of God

Have you ever looked at children and wondered how on earth Jesus could ever have thought of them as role models for the kingdom of heaven? Well, keep looking at them, then look again and again.

Children can be a wonderful reflection of God – sometimes it just takes us a while to notice. Often, as leaders, we become so convinced that we need to see children falling to their knees in repentance or verbally declaring their love for the sacrificial Lamb of God, that we fail to notice that Michael has changed from being rude and disobedient into being slightly more co-operative and kind! We might not have noticed that Bethany cleared up of her own accord this week or that George could still remember part of last week's session. These are just as much glimpses of God in the children's lives as a passionate, intellectual grasp of the gospel message.

Every one unique

So watch for glimpses of God and be encouraged by them. Pray for the children in your group now, making a note of any glimpses of God you may have overlooked before.

Glimpse 1_____

_____

Glimpse 2_____

_____

Glimpse 3_____

_____

Glimpse 4_____

_____

Glimpse 5_____

_____

Write the name of each child in your group in one or more of these categories, or invent categories to suit:

The lonely ones _____

_____

The noisy ones _____

_____

The shy ones _____

_____

The clingy ones _____

_____

The happy one _____

_____

Those who find it difficult to join in

_____

_____

Those who find it hard to take turns

_____

_____

Those who want to know Jesus but do not quite know what to do about it

_____

_____

Those who are eager to hear God's word _____

_____

Now pray for yourself and your other leaders, and your relationship with each of these children.

Remember to thank God for each other as well and do the 'Glimpses' exercise for yourself too.

A partnership with God

'The first time I met Katherine I was a teenage helper at our Explorer group, over ten years ago. She was one of the lovely 10 year olds I had agreed to lead as part of a school award scheme. I count the experience of watching her grow in faith and maturity a real privilege. She has been touched by God in so many ways throughout her life.

It has been an honour to be with her through the pain of broken friendships aged 10, with her during the discomfort of changing schools at 12 and 16, the agony of her discovery at 18, that her parents were fallible, and the hurt of unrequited love aged 20. At every stage of her life we have battled together with God's view on her problems and have prayed for guidance and an answer. To watch now as she gives her life to God in service, is a wonderful joy. Working with children is a long-term job because it is about a relationship with people, but more importantly about a partnership with God'.

IN TOUCH WITH FAMILIES

Working with children in church will mean keeping their families informed. Although you do not have the same responsibilities as teachers in school, families want to know that you and your other leaders are caring for their children in much the same way.

Right from the start, get into the habit of talking to families about what you are doing in the group. Then it will be easier if you have to inform them that their child is experiencing or causing problems. This sample letter may help you with keeping families up to date.

Sample letter to families

You may be able to adapt this letter and send it to families at the beginning of each new term.

TOP TIPS FOR HELPING FAMILIES FEEL CONFIDENT

Families need to feel confident about the events, activities and care that you offer their children. Take these basic steps towards helping them be at ease with what you are doing.

• Have an 'open-door' policy so that parents know that they can pop in and see what is happening in their child's group.

• Ask parents to tell you about any special needs their child may have, such as wearing glasses (some children will try to leave them off when their parents are not around), or any medical conditions such as asthma or diabetes.

• Chat to parents informally when you meet them in church, or when they collect their children.

• Give plenty of notice about events to ensure they do not clash with other commitments and so that parents can make necessary arrangements to bring and collect children.

News!

Name of group _____

Our group meets at _____

This term we are learning about _____

We shall also be _____

And there's something else that's pretty exciting just now

_____

If you would like to know more about any aspect of what we do as a group, please contact _____

From
(Name of overall leader of the group)

IN TOUCH WITH THE REST OF THE CHURCH

Think of a huge ocean liner leaving port. As it moves away from the quayside it is flanked by small but powerful tugs which guide it through the difficult channels. When the ship reaches open water the tugs turn back to port and the liner sails on alone. In the same way, as your work with children begins, support from church leaders and friends may be strong but, after a while, people may 'turn back' and leave you to go on alone.

It is vital to have the church continuing to support you and the other leaders *throughout* your work. They may do this through prayer and in practical ways. Your vicar or minister needs to know what you are doing in the group too. Ask him or her to meet you and the other leaders at least every couple of months, so that everyone is clear about the situation and you can ask for support in relevant areas.

Remember that the children's work is the work of the whole church. *You* may be the people doing the work week by week, but the responsibility for the children's growth as members of the church family lies with the church as a whole.

 **Helping them to know more**

If you are unsure what your church needs to know about your children's work, tick any items in the following list that apply to your situation:

The rest of the church...

☐ knows how the groups are divided up

☐ knows what the children are doing in their groups

☐ has grasped one specially exciting thing that has happened in the group recently

☐ knows of one special need that we have at present

☐ prays for the children's work

☐ asks leaders how the work is going

☐ asks the children about what they are doing in their groups

☐ gives the children opportunities to share their learning with everyone else, in church as a display or by asking them to help lead corporate worship

☐ meets with the children at occasions other than services e.g. for church social events

If you left any boxes empty, talk to your vicar or minister about these issues and how, together, you could resolve them.

 ### For all to see...

Use part of a learning session to put together something for display in your church, to let everyone see what your group is doing. How about a display of recent creative output, or photos of the children learning and having fun? You could invite a church member in to take the photos.

Children's work update

At regular intervals, consider completing a form like the one below, to give to your vicar, minister or children's work co-ordinator. Photos of the group in action willl help them to know what is happening.

Of course, if you already meet regularly with these people, such a system may be unnecessary, although you could still fill it in and distribute it to the church council or prayer group.

Whatever method you prefer, good, regular communication about children's work is vital.

Date

October – November

Group

Scramblers (3-5s)

Leaders

Angela, Tim, Margaret

Current theme

Miracles of Jesus

Range of regular activities

Play dough, Drawing, Singing, Games

Other events

A party is planned for the end of this term, jointly with the 5-7s group.

We are planning to bake some bread together for the story of the feeding of the 5000.

Outcome

The leaders are beginning to get to know the new children.

The children are beginning to understand that Jesus is someone very special.

Significant happenings and signs of progress

The children are really keen to come each week — some are reluctant to return to their parents at the end!

Laura, aged 4, asked how Jesus made water into wine, because it wasn't magic, was it. One of our teenage helpers explained that we do not know how he did it, but because Jesus is God's son, he is very powerful and can do anything, especially things to help other people.

Dreaming dreams

At this stage it would be good to feel that you have settled into a routine that works for your group. However, it is also important to keep thinking about the future by reminding yourselves frequently of your vision for children's work.

At your next leaders' meeting, use the diagram below to help you think what you would like to see happening in your group over the next six months. The thinking is based, once again, on Colossians 1:28 which you might consider the ultimate aim for children's work. Think about what is achievable, but don't be afraid to dream because God works far beyond the humanly 'achievable'!

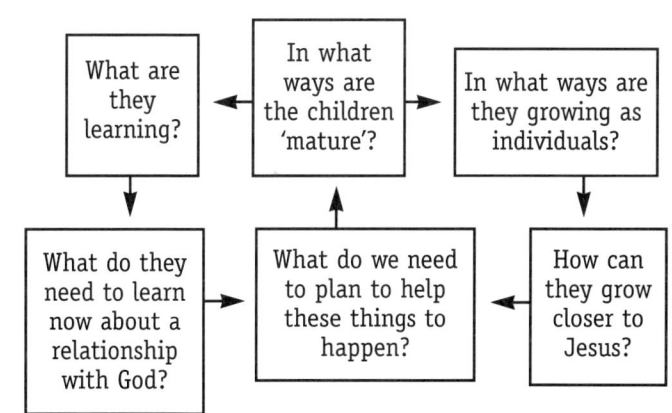

IN TOUCH WITH OTHER LEADERS

As leaders it is important to keep communicating. Get together at least once a month (in addition to your regular preparation time) to talk about how the group is going and about what you believe God is doing in the group – the big picture. Meeting together to discuss and pray encourages each other and allows everyone to express any particular needs they have. We all need to be appreciated, so use the opportunity to affirm each other, and share constructive feedback, as well as problems. The best way to do that is with a phrase such as: ' You did (X) well. It would be even more effective if...'

Looking back

This checklist will help you to think about meeting your own needs as leaders, and also those of the children in your group. However, it is not meant to induce feelings of guilt or inadequacy! Tick the relevant boxes and add comments individually first, before comparing your answers.

1 As leaders, are we managing to meet together for discussion and prayer at least once a month?

☐ Yes ☐ No ♦ Comment _____

_____

2 Do we meet regularly as leaders to plan and prepare teaching sessions?

☐ Yes ☐ No ♦ Comment _____

_____

3 Do we feel adequately supported by the rest of the church in our work?

☐ Yes ☐ No ♦ Comment _____

_____

4 Do the children know what is acceptable behaviour in the group?

☐ Yes ☐ No ♦ Comment _____

_____

5 Are any of the group activities too hard for the children?

☐ Yes ☐ No ♦ Comment _____

_____

6 Are any of the group activities too easy for the children?

☐ Yes ☐ No ♦ Comment _____

_____

7 Do the children know other adult church members apart from the group leaders?

☐ Yes ☐ No ♦ Comment _____

_____

8 Do we and the children have opportunities to talk together about ourselves and our interests?

☐ Yes ☐ No ♦ Comment _____

_____

9 Do the children seem to enjoy coming to the group?

☐ Yes ☐ No ♦ Comment _____

_____

Big praying

Pray now for your group and its leaders, bearing in mind the things that you are currently doing and those you would like to do. Ask God to help you to plan ahead and to work through all that you do.

Lord, we pray for the children (mention them individually by name)

Please help us with all the different activities we do together each week, especially...

We thank you especially for... We pray about the difficulties with...

We pray too for our leaders (each team member pray for the person on their right by name)

Give us, Lord, the wisdom to lead,

the courage to move forward,

the words to speak about you

and the grace to teach the children by the way we live.

For Jesus' sake,

Amen.

IN TOUCH WITH YOURSELF

You grow as a leader at the same time as your group develops its own nature and the individuals within it change. So stretch yourself!

New targets

Give yourself some new targets to reach this month. Tick the box as you meet each challenge.

☐ You know the full names of all the children in your group.

☐ You know where some of them live.

☐ You know the children's families, at least by sight.

☐ You have let the children's families know what you are doing this term.

☐ You have made sure that the children know the names of all the leaders, helpers and other children in the group.

☐ You have been clear with the children about the reason why the group exists.

☐ You meet regularly with your other leaders to plan and pray.

☐ Your own prayer and Bible exploration are not being neglected.

☐ You spend quality time preparing teaching sessions.

If you have not achieved all of these so far, don't panic! Some will only happen gradually, but be aware that they do need to happen.

Taking in as well as giving out

As a leader who is always giving out physically, emotionally, mentally and spiritually, you need to check where your 'input' is coming from. If your 'output' (or sessions with children) drains you more quickly than your 'input' (the Bible teaching you receive and your own time with God) can keep up, you will quickly dry up and be useless. Imagine an open teapot standing under a running tap, but tilted to pour. There is a steady flow from the spout as the pot is replenished by clean, fresh water.

You may feel that you get enough input from your group preparation. Perhaps the fellowship you enjoy with your group and the learning you do together is enough to keep you going most of the time. If so, that is good, but do not neglect opportunities to benefit from other, less demanding, times of fellowship.

Ask yourself two questions:

• Before I was a leader where did my input come from?

_____

_____

•As a leader, where does my input come from now?

_____

_____

Compare your answers. Is there any difference between them? Are you happy with the way it has worked out since you began leading the group?

Training or straining?

Consider getting some training for yourself and your other leaders. It can help you find the extra vision, energy and confidence to keep going. There may be an aspect of children's ministry that you feel you would like to do better, or you may need some new ideas about something which has become 'second nature' to you and risks being dull and repetitive. CPAS and Scripture Union are there to help you with the training you need (see *More Tools* on page 48).

If your groups are members of the Youth and Children Division of CPAS, the annual membership fee includes training on an expenses-only basis. If your children's groups are not part of the scheme, you can still contact CPAS to request training, but it will cost a higher fee.

'Drinking in' from the Bible

Our learning from the Bible is the best and most vital ongoing training we can have. So from where might our Bible training come? Here are some possibilities. If any are new to you, find out more about them and try them out. They might be ways that will fit in well with your lifestyle.

On your own Try individual quiet times or perhaps more 'strenuous' Bible study. There are many published Bible notes and commentaries available (see *More Tools* on page 48). Have a go at a new style of exploring the Bible if the guide you are using just now seems rather dull.

In church Enjoy corporate worship, fellowship, sermons, tapes, and books from the bookstall or library. If you do not manage to get to church each week, ask someone to record the service. Then you will be able to join in with it at a more suitable time.

Small groups You may have home groups, Bible study groups and support networks from which to choose. If your church does not have small groups, perhaps you could start one, with your church leader's permission. Your other children's leaders may appreciate it too!

Other Christians Learn to rely on friends, prayer partners, and a mentor or spiritual director. Really value your Christian friends – they're worth their weight in gold!

Nationally, regionally or locally organized training events or conferences Do you ever have the chance to get away and spend a day, a weekend or even a week focusing on God? Try it – you won't regret it! For details of training events and conferences for children's leaders, contact CPAS on (01926) 334242 or Scripture Union on (01908) 856000.

IMPORTANT ISSUES

A question that voluntary leaders of children's groups often ask is: 'How far am I responsible for the welfare of the children with whom I work?' This 'pocket' will offer guidance on this difficult subject so that you feel more confident in dealing with some of the issues that affect the children in your group.

TIME TO CARE

'Surely we have enough work to do with preparing sessions and getting resources ready, without searching around for personal problems to sort out!' Yes, there is some truth in that view, but children bring problem 'baggage' with them which will affect the way they relate, behave and respond in our groups.

The Christian is commanded to help anyone in need in exactly the way they need it. So we have no choice but to help the children in our group with the difficulties that present themselves during teaching sessions or in casual conversations elsewhere. The effects of bullying, divorce and the death of a grandparent or pet, the trauma of moving house or school, or of having a new baby brother or sister all come with them to our group. For most children, we shall probably never know just how heavy is the 'baggage' that they are carrying.

'750,000 British children have no contact with their fathers, following the breakdown of marital relationships.'

(From a report by *The Family Policies Study Centre Survey of Lone Parents*, partly reproduced in *What on Earth are we doing to our Children?* published by Marantha Community, 1995.)

'10,000 children telephone 'Childline' for help every day.'

(From *The Times*, 7.1.95.)

Flashback

Work through these questions about your own childhood:

- Who were the most important people in your life?
- Which were the most important places to you?

- What was your biggest worry when you were a child?

- What excited you most?

- What did you find especially hard to do?

Now think about a child in your group that you know well. Try to answer these questions for him or her. Did any answers turn out to be the same for both of you?

No generalizations

In terms of the issues they face, we cannot generalize about children. Each child is unique and this means that we may encounter different issues that face different children. Because children are very vulnerable to external influences and, at an early age, are unable to disguise their effects on them, we may see marked changes in their behaviour, relationships and responses, in a relatively short space of time.

'The person who first asserted that "your school days are the happiest days of your life" was very fortunate. A lot of children, even the very young, are struggling with anxieties and conflicts of emotion at this time.'

(From *It's Tough Being an Infant* by Irene Brown, published by Scripture Union, 1996.)

Different ages, different issues

As children grow up, different issues will affect them at different stages. Some will influence all children at some point, whilst others will never be part of a child's experience.

Decide which of the following issues could influence the children in your group. Also consider how each might affect both the individual child and also the group as a whole.

arguments/fighting at home • bullying • divorce • moving school • moving house • bodily changes • a new baby at home • going up to the next school year • death of a grandparent • dental brace • having to wear glasses • death of a pet • a parent returning to work • a new 'mum' or 'dad' • illness of a family member • moving up to a new school • a friend moving away • a parent losing a job

At least some of these issues will affect the children in your group. With your other leaders, think through in advance how you might accommodate children who behave in an unusual way or who find they need to talk to a leader about the strange things that are happening to them.

Taking care

Here are some ways of making sure that you do not overlook any children who are facing difficult situations and who need help:

• Talk and listen to the children – they will probably tell you about their home, family and feelings.

• Talk to the children's families about them, but take care not to read too much into what they say.

• Make sure that the children know they are accepted in the group, however they feel.

• If children are unwilling to join in an activity, do not force them – offer an alternative or make sure an adult keeps an eye on them.

• Remember that your group may be the only place that offers any stability for some children, so keep things as normal as possible.

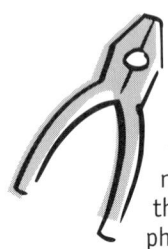

Photo prayers

Pray now for any group members who are facing particular issues just now. Be specific. Write their names or put a photo of them in a prominent place, to remind yourself to keep on praying.

Taking it further

Occasionally you may feel you need to talk to your vicar or minister about a particular child's situation, either for the sake of the individual or because it is adversely affecting the life of the whole group. Ideally you will have this discussion with the consent of the child's parent or guardian, but this may not always be possible or appropriate. Remember, however, that you are only responsible for the children in your group while they are in your care.

'If there is not a place where tears are understood,

Where can I go to cry?

If there is not a place where my spirit can take wing,

Where do I go to fly?

If there is not a place where my questions can be asked,

Where do I go to seek?

If there is not a place where my feelings can be heard,

Where can I go to speak?

If there is not a place where I can try and learn and grow,

Where can I just be me?'

(Author unknown)

Keeping records

Keep a record card for each child in your group. It could include basic information such as name, address and birthday. Be careful of writing comments about children that you would not wish someone else to see.

Here is an example of one which you could photocopy and use, or adapt as you think necessary.

Record sheet

Full name _____

Preferred name _____

Age _____

_____

Address _____

_____

Telephone number _____

Name of parent or guardian _____

Point of contact within the church (e.g.parent) _____

Point of contact in case of emergency _____

_____

Details of any medical condition or disability _____

_____

_____

Any special needs regarding learning (e.g. dyslexia, wears spectacles)

_____

_____

Other information _____

_____

_____

Of course, though essentially confidential, such a record form would be made available to the main leaders of a group (that is, those aged eighteen and over). Parents are also entitled to see it on request. Used within these guidelines, a set of record cards is a sensible and useful precaution.

It is just possible that you are the only person praying for the children in your group.

Pray!

MORE THAN A BUILDING

'We long to see children in church, but of course, it is not the building we are concerned about, it is the people *inside* it – God's people, the body of Christ. We want children to be recognized as a vital part of the body. Then they will learn the value of meeting with others to worship God, develop their gifts and begin a lifetime of Christian service.

CHILDREN WELCOME?

For many children, church is a place to which they have never been or where they do not feel welcome. In your imagination, look around your church and ask yourself 'What is there here that is welcoming to children?' Have you thought of anything? If you are still not sure, just ask yourself how many things are at a child's eye level or at a child's height, or how many notices are addressed to children or at least acknowledge them.

If we want children in our churches, we need to make them welcome. This will involve some creative planning and preparation in advance, like rearranging the furniture or providing a special place for the children to sit so that they can see what is going on. Can you imagine the vicar asking adults to sit on chairs designed for children? So why should children have to put up with second best? Our churches should be the most welcoming place in the entire community – even, or perhaps especially, for children.

'Our underlying attitudes to the value and status of our children will be reflected in the welcome we give them. If we believe children have a right to be in church and are significant already because of God's

love for them, then that belief should be reflected in our attitudes, values and practical planning. If we actually believe this, then not only those who welcome at the door, but other adults and service leaders should begin to treat the children as fellow-members, rather than awkward nuisances who have to be provided for, because they happen to be there.'

(From *Seen and Heard* by Jackie Cray, published by Kingsway, 1994.)

Child-friendly church?

Look at the following list of statements to help you to think about your own church's welcome to children. Tick those at which you think your church is good:

☐ The adults in church talk to the children.

☐ When children enter the building they are ignored, but someone greets their parents.

☐ The children are included in the welcome at the beginning of the service.

☐ The first words addressed to the children in the service are not 'It's time for you to go out to your groups now...'

☐ There is evidence around of the children's involvement in church life, such as posters advertising children's events and information about children's groups.

☐ The vicar or minister talks to the children informally before or after the service.

☐ People use the children's names when speaking to them individually.

The statements reflect fairly routine occurrences in many places, and indicate our attitude towards children as a church. How would we greet the Queen if she arrived at the door? Ignore her? Talk only to her mother and say, 'Does your daughter need a hymn book?' Is the Queen more important than the children who come to our churches? Discuss this with your other leaders.

Spend a couple of minutes thinking together about everything in your church that would make children feel welcome. Got some ideas? Good! Write them in the church below!

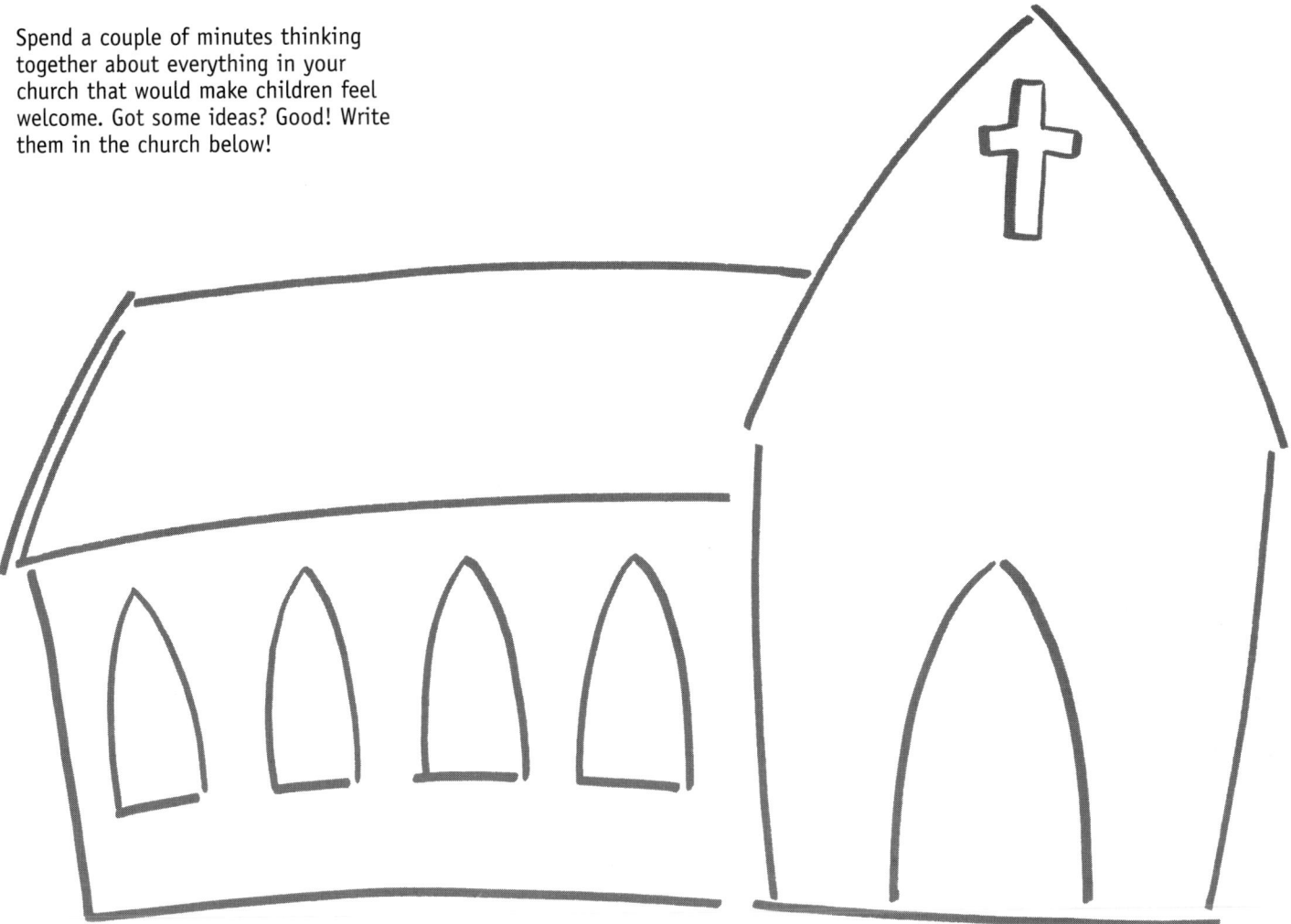

'A child's attitude to church can be affected by what happens in those first few moments after entering the building. Many children feel they are not coming voluntarily. As far as they are concerned they are there because their parents want them to be there. Their experience tells them that church is a place where adults come first... The child's impression is reinforced when adults greet one another warmly, exchange news and pass on messages without even once turning to the children and welcoming or including them. Be honest, if you went somewhere several times and were never spoken to personally, or people only referred to you in a secondary sort of way, would you want to go again?'

(From *Seen and Heard* by Jackie Cray, published by CPAS/Monarch, 1994.)

It is easy to be negative when children and church are put together. Instead, try to be encouraged by the things which *are* good news for children, such as a friendly congregation, good children's groups or a vicar who welcomes children enthusiastically.

No church is completely child-friendly or completely child-deterring, but we need to be creative and develop the good things we are doing so that they keep on happening and getting better. Do not leave things to chance. If the children feel welcome when they come through the door or enjoy the parts of the service at which they are present, find out *why* so that you can keep doing it and then improve it beyond all recognition!

'I like laughing at church... I like it when Beverley makes us laugh.'

Natalie aged 8

'It's fun when you get a chance to say thanks to God.'

James aged 6

AFTER THE WELCOME, WHAT?

Of course, having children in church is not just about making them feel welcome in services – we are responsible for helping them to be part of the living, worshipping body of Christ. Once we have the welcome right, we need to think about what the children are actually *doing* in church. Are they just going to sit and listen to the service while the adults get on with it? Will they be able to join in and lead some parts of it? Will there be parts that involve them physically? How much will the service enable them to develop their relationship with God? This last point is vital – we should always remember that children are spiritual beings who need opportunities to respond to God and to allow him to speak to them. This is crucial to the development of a child's faith.

Near-death experience

'Our church is an inner-city parish church which, ten years ago, was "near to death". A new vicar came whose vision was to develop a church made up from the local community, and much work was done in those initial years to come alongside local people and show them that Jesus was someone who loved them and was relevant to their lives.

The vicar arrived with his two small children, so right from the start young children were part of this "new" congregation which was focused on the morning service. A traditional evening service was maintained for those who, through their perseverance and faith, had kept our church in existence.

We try to make children feel welcome by saying "hello" and finding out their names; people in church don't tend to "shush" or frown at the children. We then tell them about the children's groups and someone will invite them personally to one. If they want to go, that person will take them to the appropriate group and introduce them to the leader. When the children come in from the groups, we encourage them to show us the things that they have been doing, and we round off the service together.'

Jan, outreach worker.

Children in church services

How can you make church a valuable experience for children? There is no easy route, but if you do not try, children will not be valued in it. The following suggestions are not a key to instant success, but are important elements in making church services meaningful and welcoming for children.

Think about language If there are words that children will not understand, explain them or find another way of saying what is meant.

Have opportunities for everyone to respond to God, either in prayer or praise or silence, or in some other way, and encourage the children to use the opportunity too.

Give children opportunities to be involved in helping with services They could have a go at cleaning, hand out books, set out the furniture and welcome people into church, for instance. However, do not *force* them to do these things.

Have a balance of items in the service that are aimed at either adults or children You cannot please everyone all the time, but you can aim at different ages at different points in a service. For example, try prayers that are targeted at children, and a sermon that speaks to adults but which has visual aids that children can enjoy.

Think about how long items take We cannot expect children to concentrate on one thing for fifteen minutes – many adults have trouble doing that! Adjust things to keep everyone feeling involved.

There are many books of ideas for all-age worship including sketches, stories, quizzes and songs so you will not find an encyclopaedic list of ideas here. However, here are some thoughts about children and adults worshipping together which are worth bearing in mind:

• We would not force *adults* to lead something in a service, so do not force children either.

• All the preparation for the service will be wasted if no one can hear what the person who is leading says.

• Let children do things at which they are good, or let them try something for the first time and be understanding if it does not go quite as expected. They need to use and develop their gifts, so talk to them afterwards about how their contribution went.

• Give everyone opportunities to respond to God.

• Children need to know that they are really contributing to worship, not just enjoying or providing 'entertainment'. Do not give them the impression that they are practising for when they can take part 'properly'.

• Do not expect adults to do things which make them feel childish, nor expect children to become adults for the duration of a service.

• Do not avoid silence. An all-age service does not have to be noisy.

God likes us to have fun.

'The children help to welcome people into church and give out books and service sheets. Some of the songs are fast and loud, with clapping and the children playing instruments like maracas, bells and drums. Some of the songs have a lot of silence for people to listen to God. The children help by taking up the water, bread and wine for Communion, doing Bible readings, acting in plays, setting out the cups for coffee, saying prayers and tidying up at the end.

There is a time in the service for sharing news and we sing 'Happy Birthday' to people who have had their birthday that week. Sometimes we have games like guessing which Bible character someone is describing, or working out mixed-up Bible characters' names. Also there is a chance to say 'hello' to others and to say 'Peace be with you' and you can carry on talking when you have a drink and biscuit at the end. A lot of the adults are good fun and like to have us around. They talk to us and ask us about what we've been doing.

Nobody minds when things go wrong – we like to laugh in the service because God likes us to have fun. I know that God is in our service and the singing and the prayers help us to get close to him'.

As well as in services, children need opportunities to be part of other aspects of church life too and to get to know the other members of the family. Then, in years to come when the children leave our groups, they will not feel like strangers in their own church. If we constantly keep them separate from the rest of the church, we shall soon see the last of them.

GROWING CHILDREN FOR LEADERSHIP

Try to think back to the time when you first started to prepare for your children's group. How straightforward was it to find leaders? Perhaps your preparation was made easier because there were already people available in your church to help begin the work. If not, how much easier would it have been if there *had* been? Part of the difficulty of leading children's groups is actually finding people to lead them. Why are there so few people in our churches trained and ready to do it?

Perhaps it is because many people do not know what their gifts are. As we discovered in **Pocket 1**, *you* have gifts – yes, honestly, you have! Your willingness to be involved in children's work is a powerful gift in itself, and by now you may well be aware of others. Pause to think back to how you found out about and developed your gifts and which people, places and opportunities were involved.

Children have gifts

Children also have important gifts, although they may still be undeveloped. You can probably think of children who play instruments, draw well, are skilled in befriending other children, or who always seem to be encouraging others. Some may feel they are not good at anything. They need your encouragement to identify their gifts and your help to have the opportunities to try them out. Yes, it is risky, but these children will soon be the leaders in the church. They need room to develop the gifts God has given them.

Paul talks about the use of gifts in the church in Romans 12:4-8. He encourages the members of the church in Rome to use whatever gifts they have (vs6-8). Let this encourage you to be bold about using your gifts too and about helping children to grow theirs.

Identifying gifts

By now, you have perhaps started to think about your group and to identify gifts that the children in your group have. If not, try to work out what each of the children enjoy doing or are good at. For example, you may have children who particularly enjoy singing or drama, or who are good at craftwork, reading aloud or explaining things to others.

Over the next few weeks, identify one gift in each child in your group and write their name into the chart below. Then consider how you can encourage these gifts in your group and in the life of the rest of the church.

Singing and music

Art and craft

Reading aloud

Explaining things

Making friends

Praying

Using and growing gifts

Having identified some of the children's gifts, look through the following ways of using them in church. Tick any activities in which you think the children could be involved. Discuss with your other leaders how you could allow time for the children to begin exercising their gifts in these ways.

☐ Reading in church.

☐ Telling a story in church or in the group.

☐ Praying in corporate worship.

☐ Encouraging others.

☐ Making friends with new group members.

☐ Making resources for use in corporate worship.

☐ Singing in corporate worship.

☐ Writing prayers, stories, songs or poems.

☐ Welcoming people.

☐ Cooking or baking for church events.

☐ Explaining ideas to others.

☐ Designing and drawing resources.

☐ Other. _____

Children praying for each other

Jeremy Brown is a children's worker in an inner-city church. He runs two home groups, to which he invites children from church families who attend the Sunday activities on a regular basis. One of the groups is for children at infant school, and the other caters for juniors.

All the children are encouraged to pray for each other. Jeremy asks the younger group for suggestions, then gives any children who want to pray, a specific topic to pray about. Having been told what to do and when to do it, they are quite happy to pray aloud for each other's needs.

With the older group, the approach is less structured, and the children discuss what God might want them to pray for in a particular situation. They are encouraged to share needs and pray for each other more personally. Jeremy has seen the children's faith develop as they have learnt to trust God to answer their prayers – exciting stuff!

Children need opportunities to use their gifts as early as possible. In school they soon begin to use their skills to explore the world and to present their findings – in other words, to be active and involved. The idea is that children will continually develop skills which enable them to take on increasingly difficult tasks and, ultimately, to become leaders in the world.

This should be our thinking in church too: to develop children's gifts *now* so that they can take on roles of leadership and service.

At the beginning of this 'pocket', you thought about finding a ready-made team to take on the children's work in your church. If this team is not yet available, perhaps it could be one day if your church has discovered ways of developing the gifts of those who are currently growing up in it. Otherwise, you will forever be plugging gaps and trying to persuade people to take on the work. This gap-plugging exercise may give the impression that being involved in children's ministry must be the worst job in the world. That would be a shame. Actually we know it is one of the *best!*

'I think it's more important to do things for God than things for yourself.'

James, aged six

Imagine that you lead a group of 3-6 year olds, and there is no other children's work in the church. What will you do in eighteen months' time when the six-year-old is eight and the youngest is still only four? Can you cope with such a wide age range in the group? Should you keep the same group going but try to make the activities suitable for all the ages, or should you leave the eight-year-old to fend for herself in church? Or should the church think about starting a new group for the sake of one child?

Suppose you and your group of 7-11 year olds get on fantastically well together. *They* stimulate your teaching and learning about God; *you* are helping them to make huge leaps of faith on which everyone is commenting with great pleasure. Not unnaturally, two of the children become twelve. They do not want to move up, and if you are honest, neither do you want them to. Will you hang on to them rather than moving them up into Pathfinders?

As the months go by, the children in your group will get to know each other and learn to trust you and the other leaders. This is brilliant – making good relationships is a key aspect of children's ministry. However, eventually they will need to leave your group and move up to a new one. Some will be ready for it, and will enjoy getting to know new leaders and facing the challenge of new activities; others may be reluctant to move up; one or two may decide to stay in church with their family or stop coming to church altogether. It can all become very complicated.

In this 'pocket', we shall look both at what to do if there is no other group into which your children can move up, and also at how to help them move up if there *is* one.

No group to move up to

If there is nowhere for them to go, you may feel you can keep the older children in your group without neglecting the younger ones. However, it would be more normal for you to think of letting the older ones go so that you can concentrate on the majority who still fall within the specified age range of the group.

Ideally, before you get to this stage, your church should reflect on how highly it values the presence of children in it, and should decide how to provide nurture for the older children. Together you may try to recruit leaders in order to start a new group for them, or restructure services so that you can meet the needs of those who are not now part of a group.

In the meantime, it is important to involve the older children in one of the following ways:

• invite them to help with a children's group;

• plan with your other leaders to structure teaching sessions so that you can include the older ones at their level, for example by organizing activities that present more of a challenge to them, or by asking a leader to concentrate on working specifically with them.

Of course, neither option is ideal, but attempting one of them may mean the difference between a child staying with the group or leaving the church.

Talk to your vicar, minister or children's work co-ordinator about the possibility of a group for older children, and see that planning begins. Someone will need to recruit leaders and find suitable premises. Remember, though, that it is not automatically *your* job to set up a new group – it is the responsibility of the whole church.

NO DESIRE TO MOVE UP

In **Pocket 7** we thought about wanting children to develop and grow within the church. Ideally, they will move smoothly through each group that is available to them showing signs of increasing maturity as they go. We shall be pleased that they are eager to move on and are flourishing in their new groups. Realistically, however, this will not always be the case, and there may be many reasons why not.

Children may be going through other changes like moving into a new school year, and need some stability; they may be worried about getting on with new leaders, particularly if they are young children who are moving from a group lead by female leaders to one that has male leaders; they may be unsure about going into a group in which there are much older children – imagine a seven-year-old, the eldest in his group, suddenly becoming the youngest in a group that has tough eleven-year-olds in it.

I'm glad I wasn't on my own

'When me and Becky and Michael were told that we were going to leave the 5-7s group and go into the 8-11s group we were a bit scared. We liked it in our group and we didn't want to go up because some of the children in the next group are a lot older than us and also we didn't know the leaders. I was glad that I wasn't moving up on my own, but I'd rather have stayed in the other group.

When it got near the time to move up, one Sunday two of the leaders from the 8-11s group came and joined in with us. We did lots of games and some drama with them and it was really good. They came to our group again another time and then we went to see their group one Sunday and joined in when they had a story. But we felt like we knew the leaders and we thought our group was a bit babyish for us when we went back.'

Smoothing the move

Surprise, surprise – there are no easy answers, but some of the following may help:

• Ask a leader to move up to the next group *with* the children if they are facing other big life-changes at the same time. This need only be for a half-term or term. A leader from the group above may consider swapping places, to cover for this piece of creative planning.

• Involve some leaders from the next group in your activities before the time to move up. This will give the older children an opportunity to get to know new faces.

• Arrange a session during which those who are due to move up can talk about their concerns.

• Pass on information to the new group leaders about the children who are moving up so that they get to know their particular needs.

• With the leaders of the next group up, explore the possibility of that group going away together for a residential weekend, to help the younger ones mix with the older ones and therefore to settle in more quickly.

LOOKING BACK

You made it – the end of your first year! Not surprisingly, it is time to look back thankfully and to look ahead enthusiastically – and, of course, to organize a massive group celebration!

Ask your vicar, minister or children's work co-ordinator to work through this 'pocket' with you and your other leaders, as a way of doing with you what will hopefully become an annual review.

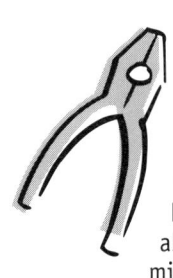

Faithful One

Thank God now for his faithfulness to your group. Stay silent for a few minutes, and allow him to speak to you about anything you have missed in your own recollections.

One-year-old celebrations

• Organize a service (or part of a service) to celebrate all that has happened in your group. Include the fun times, things you have made, places you have visited and all that the children have learnt about themselves and God.

• In your next session together, have a party. The children could make food to bring and you could have prizes for each child.

• In church present certificates or prizes for being part of the group.

• Make 'group birthday' cakes for everyone to eat after a service.

FIRST THE GOOD NEWS

Recently you may have found it hard to step back from the group and find reasons to be encouraged. What went disastrously wrong or how few children turned up on Sunday will probably weigh heavily on your mind, whilst you will have let your major successes pass relatively unnoticed. Well, you need to put that right for a start!

Try to recall some of the positive and encouraging things that have happened in your group during the last year – for instance, the sessions in which children asked questions eagerly (a sign that they meant business with learning about God), or the times when you all had fun together playing a game and the group really gelled. Remember the children individually and all that God has done in their lives – be encouraged by even the smallest sign of growth. Think of the times when the children were made to feel a vital and valued part of the church.

Write here as much as you can, and share your thoughts with your other leaders as soon as possible.

Now the new ways

At the end of your first year's experience of running the group, try to find new ways of handling those aspects of your group's life which have become stale or difficult. The following framework may help. Again, try to answer the questions individually first, then compare your answers.

1 Do you have the right number of leaders for the group?

☐ Yes ☐ No   Comment _____

_____

_____

2 Is the place where your group meets still suitable for the children?

☐ Yes ☐ No   Comment _____

_____

_____

3 Are there gaps in your programme? For example, do you have enough social time or enough Bible exploration?

☐ Yes ☐ No   Comment _____

_____

_____

4 Does your group actively participate in the life of the church?

☐ Yes ☐ No   Comment _____

_____

_____

5 Have any new children joined the group?

☐ Yes ☐ No   Comment _____

_____

_____

If so, what do you think attracted them?

_____

_____

6 Have any children left the group?

☐ Yes ☐ No   Comment _____

_____

_____

If so, do you know why?

_____

_____

7 If you are using a published teaching resource, is it still suitable for your group?

☐ Yes ☐ No   Comment _____

_____

_____

8 To maintain a balanced group programme, which of the following do you think you should be doing more of?

Tick as many as you like.

☐ Teaching from the Old Testament.

☐ Teaching from the New Testament.

☐ Chatting to members in order to build good relationships.

☐ Games.

☐ Fun sessions such as quizzes.

☐ Drama.

☐ Singing.

☐ Other creative uses of music.

☐ Session at which you invite other church members to speak or do something special.

☐ Family sessions.

☐ Craft activities.

☐ Involvement in church services.

☐ Social activities.

☐ Other. _____

_____

☐ Other. _____

_____

And now for the future

As well as basing some changes on aspects of your group's life that have become stale or difficult, it is vital to plan for the next twelve months by refreshing your idea of where you believe God wants your group to go. This will involve sticking with your overall aim (see page 00), but perhaps changing the emphasis slightly. Then your children's work will stay exciting and relevant.

Consider these questions and try to think big. Go on, be daring!

• Put your aim into different words, stressing the new emphasis that you believe you need to have next year.

_____

_____

• So what do you think God wants your children to be like this time next year?

_____

_____

• So what would you like to *do* with your group over the next twelve months that you are not currently doing?

_____

_____

• In what ways would you like to see your group actively participating in the life of the church this time next year?

_____

_____

• What change might all this require in you as a team of leaders?

_____

_____

• What might be the catalyst for bringing this change about?

_____

_____

Now, before you forget all your good ideas, think how these changes might be achieved. What practical things do you need to make them start to happen?

☐ More money.

☐ A bigger room.

☐ More leaders.

☐ Further training for leaders.

☐ Better equipment.

☐ More committed prayer support

☐ Other _____

_____

How could you get these things?

_____

_____

Who might help you to get them?

_____

_____

Well, you have rummaged through the 'pockets' of this 'toolbag' pretty thoroughly by now. There is not much left for us to do now except to say 'Thank you! You're doing a very important job!'

Working with children is one of the most crucial tasks in the church. You and people like you are helping to equip the church with its most valuable resource – mature Christians who will pass on the message of good news to others both now and also in the years ahead.

Be encouraged in everything you do. Even when children respond blankly, 'I don't understand...', take it as a sign that they *want* to understand; when they demand, 'I want to know more...', try to be joyful rather than wishing they would go away and leave you alone!

Take encouragement from Paul when he says:

> 'We proclaim him, admonishing and teaching everyone with all wisdom, so that we may present everyone perfect in Christ. To this end I labour, struggling with all his energy, which so powerfully works in me.'
>
> Colossians 1:28-29

It may be a struggle sometimes, but God will give us his strength when we ask him. We will not always get it right, but God will do his work through us in spite of the mistakes we make. Even in the most uninspiring teaching sessions, you could be changing lives for ever.

Reading her Bible in bed

Alison, aged ten, does not come from a church family, but goes regularly to a mid-week club attached to the church. Out of the blue, in a conversation with her group leader, she suddenly said, 'Psalm 136 keeps saying, "his love is eternal", doesn't it?'

When the leader asked how she knew that it did, her reply was, 'Oh I was reading my Bible in bed last night.'

'Give thanks to the Lord, because he is good; his love is eternal.'

Psalm 136:1

MORE TOOLS

USEFUL ADDRESSES

[Publicity and tracts]
Christian Publicity Organization,
Garcia Estate, Canterbury Road,
Worthing, West Sussex BN13 1BW
Tel: 01903 264556

(Bible tape libraries)
St Helen's, Bishopsgate,
St Helen's Vestry, Great Helen's
Street, London EC3A 6AT

Anchor Recordings, 72 The Street,
Kennington, Ashford,
Kent TN24 9HS

(Training courses for group leaders)
Youth and Children Division, CPAS,
Athena Drive, Tachbrook Park,
Warwick CV34 6NG
Tel: 01926 334242

(Help with group insurance)
Youth Clubs UK, 11 St Bride Street,
London EC4A 4AS
Tel: 0171 3532366

For cheap insurance to affiliated
youth organizations:

The Ecclesiastical Insurance Group,
Beaufort House, Brunswick Road,
Gloucester GL1 1JZ
Tel: 01452 528533

For 'youth combined policies' as well
as ordinary church policies:

Advice Development Team,
National Council for Voluntary
Organizations, Regent's Wharf,
8 All Saints Street, London N1 9RL
Tel: 0171 7136161

For details about insurance
protection for voluntary
organizations:

Association of British Insurers,
51 Gresham Street,
London EC2V 7HQ
Tel: 0171 6003333

For information about which
companies offer specific risks:

**(Help with residentials,
including insurance)**
CCI (UK), PO Box 169,
Coventry CV1 4PW
Tel: 01203 559099

(Holiday activities)
CYFA/Pathfinder Ventures Ltd,
CPAS, Athena Drive, Tachbrook Park,
Warwick CV34 6NG
Tel: 01926 334242

Scripture Union in Schools,
207-209 Queensway, Bletchley,
Milton Keynes,
Buckinghamshire MK2 2EB
Tel: 01908 856000

RESOURCES

CPAS Code	Title	Author and Publisher
	HOW-TO RESOURCES FOR LEADERS	
C18001	The Adventure Begins	Terry Clutterham, CPAS/Scripture Union
	Children in the Early Church	W.A.Strange, Paternoster
	Groups Without Frontiers	Terry Clutterham, Penny Frank, Phil Moon, CPAS
	Working with Under 6's	Val Brown, Scripture Union
	Become Like a Child (working with 5-7+)	Kathryn Copsey, Scripture Union
	Help There's a Child in My Church! (8-10+)	Peter Graystone, Scripture Union
	Reaching Children	Paul Butler, Scripture Union
C18003	Time for Children	George Lihou, CPAS
03576	Seen and Heard	Jackie Cray CPAS/Monarch
	One Hundred and One Ideas for Creative Prayers	Judith Merrell, Scripture Union
	TEACHING RESOURCES	
	SALT: Scripture Union's quarterly children's teaching programme SALT: 3-4+, SALT: 5-7+, SALT: 8-10+, SALT: 11-13+	Scripture Union
	Pic 'n' Mix (programme outlines for under 12s)	Judith Merrell, Scripture Union
	The Lion Storyteller Bible (for under 5s)	Bob Hartman, Lion Publishing
	The Family Activity Box	Sue Clutterham, Scripture Union
03585	100 Instant Children's Talks	Sue Relf, Kingsway
03673	Quiz Resource Book	Richard and Mary Chewter, Scripture Union
	DRAMA AND MUSIC RESOURCES	
	Spring Harvest Song Books	Spring Harvest
	Jump Up if You're Wearing Red	National Society/Church House Publishing
	Acting Up	Dave Hopwood, National Society/ Church House
	Telling Tales	Dave Hopwood, CPAS
	CRAFT IDEAS	
03643	Here's One I Made Earlier	Kathryn Copsey, Scripture Union
	How to Cheat at Visual Aids (Old Testament)	Judith Merrell, Scripture Union
03674	How to Cheat at Visual Aids	Judith Merrell, Scripture Union
	HOLIDAY CLUB RESOURCES	
	Going Bananas!	Sue Clutterham, Scripture Union
	Chatterbox	Andy Saunders/Kathryn Copsey, Scripture Union
	Newshounds	Peter Graystone, Scripture Union
	Nuts and Bolts – Running Holiday Clubs	Steve Hutchinson, Scripture Union
	REFLECTIVE, CREATIVE BIBLE APPROACH FOR ADULTS	
	Alive to God	Scripture Union
	Closer to God	Scripture Union

The resources with a CPAS code are available from CPAS Sales on 01926 334242 during the day, or on 01926 335855 at any other time. Email: sales@cpas.org.uk